D1783922

CONTENTS

INTRODUCTION

As I breasted the summit ridge I met the full force of the wind and pulled on an extra jersey and my anorak. It was early June yet the north facing corries were still ringed with cornices and the gullies were choked with old snow. Spring comes late to the high tops of the Scottish Highlands. Underfoot the buds of the dwarf willows were only just breaking yet below in the glen the alder, rowan and birch were in full leaf. I found a sheltered nook in the rocks near the summit cairn and opened the rucksack for lunch.

Blue smoke was rising from the slopes far below as the estate workers took advantage of the dry spell for burning heather. A pair of golden eagles, curious of my presence, soared overhead. To the west the long tongue of the sea loch led out into the Minch and waves were breaking white on a rocky reef. The remaining panorama was of mountains stretching away as far as the eye could see, black rock ridges giving way to steep heather and grass.

It was another world. I was quite alone yet completely at ease and happy in such an environment.

The aim of this guide is to encourage the reader to explore the remote mountains and glens of the Highlands and to sample such experience. He must be bold enough to leave the busy tourist centres and main roads and walk into the hills. Hill walking in Scotland is a perfectly safe undertaking if approached sensibly and this guide indicates the necessary precautions and equipment that should be taken.

There are 279 mountains in Scotland over 3,000 feet and almost all of these can be climbed without the use of ropes or specialised techniques. Even Queen Victoria climbed such formidable mountains as Ben MacDhui and Lochnagar.

This is not to say that the hills are tame, for the Highlands can provide exacting climbs and Scottish trained climbers are amongst the world's best.

The separate mountains over 3,000 feet are known as the Munros after Sir Hugh Munro who first listed them in 1891. The ascent of all the Munros provides the ultimate challenge to the Scottish hill walker and the feat has been achieved by about 120 people so far. Sir Hugh climbed them all except two and it was left to the Reverend A. E. Robertson to become the first Munroist in 1901. It is said that on the summit of his final Munro he kissed the cairn first and then his wife.

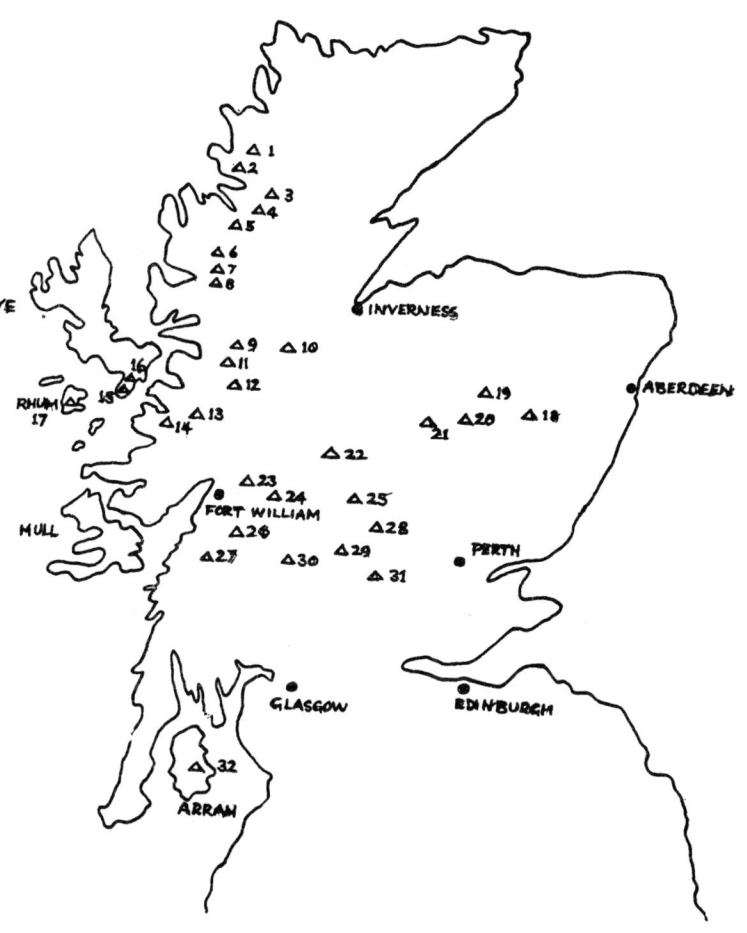

SKYE

RHUM
17

MULL

INVERNESS

ABERDEEN

FORT WILLIAM

PERTH

GLASGOW

EDINBURGH

ARRAN

△1
△2
△3
△4
△5
△6
△7
△8
△9 △10
△11
16
18
△12
△13
△14
△19
△20 △18
△21
△22
△23
△24 △25
△28
△26
△27 △30 △29
△31
△32

Ladhar Bheinn (See expedition No. 14)

Askival (See expedition No. 17)

THE HIGHLAND SCENE

The beauty of Scotland lies in the mountains, lochs, glens, forests and rivers and to experience them fully you must walk to the remote areas where the progress of man has not reached. The scenery of the high mountains has not changed much since the last ice age about ten thousand years ago.

The vegetation growth however changes with climate and 7,000 years ago, following a mild damp period, the tree line extended to a height of 2,500 feet. More recently the old forests have been ravaged by man seeking timber for houses, ships and the smelting of iron ore. The introduction of sheep and the expansion of the deer population for sport meant that the young trees were grazed and regeneration was impossible. The Forestry Commission has done much to reverse this trend but their primary function is the provision of timber and most of their trees are imported exotic species of spruce, fir and larch. The huge new pulp mill at Fort William will eventually run entirely on Scottish grown timber. The old Caledonian forest that covered most of the Highlands consisted of oak and hazel on the lower ground with alder and willow beside the streams while the upper slopes held birch, juniper and the magnificent Scots Pine. Certain areas of primeval forest do remain and have been fenced to allow for regeneration. Good examples are the east end of Glen Affric for Scots Pine and Letterewe beside Loch Maree for oak.

Not only does the scenery of the Highlands change with height but it changes dramatically from area to area. You meet a great variety of rock types each having its own characteristics. The rock structure of the highlands was one of the oldest land masses exposed anywhere in the world. The most ancient is the grey Lewisian gneiss of Sutherland and Ross-shire over 1,000 million years old. The Torridonian sandstone that has weathered to produce spectacular rock peaks such as Stac Polly and An Teallach is 600 million years old. This sandstone has been overlayed by white Cambrian quartzite on several peaks in the north west and elsewhere you will find coarse granites and sparkling mica schist. The sharp pointed Cuillin hills of Skye are comparatively recently formed; they are of black gabbro and were thrown up by volcanic activity only 50 million years ago.

For the collector the semi-precious Cairngorm stones (smoky-quartz) can occasionally be found in stream beds in the Cairngorm range. They are the traditional ornaments of Highland Dress.

FLORA AND FAUNA

The flora and fauna of the Highlands are diverse and I will only mention the most interesting species that you as a hill walker are likely to see.

The hills and glens abound in Red Deer, the stalking of which provided an immense influx of capital into the Highlands in the 19th century when deer forests were established and shooting lodges built. In winter the herds are driven down from the high tops by snow but in the summer they move up to the high plateau to feed off moss and to escape the flies. They are very timid animals and particularly wary of man but their heads can often be seen silhouetted against the sky as they watch you from a distant ridge.

For most of the year the stags and hinds live in separate herds but in the autumn the stags collect their own herds of hinds prior to the rutting season. At this time the glens are filled with the roaring of stags announcing their presence and warding off other suitors and fights are not uncommon. You may be lucky enough to pick up antlers while you are hill walking since stags lose them every year in the early summer and grow another set.

The Mountain Hare is quite common above 1,500 feet and this attractive animal can often be seen scurrying away into the rocks. The hare changes his coat to white during the winter months but an early thaw in spring can make him conspicuous and vulnerable. Once in February on Ben Lawers I heard a great commotion and squeaking and rounding a bluff of rock I saw a golden eagle trying to fly off with a mountain hare in its talons. As I approached the eagle soared away and the hare made good his escape.

Foxes make dens high up on boulder strewn slopes and I have seen them loping along narrow snow covered ridges in winter. Their warning barks are frequently heard in the glens and at night the sound carries a long way.

Wild Cat and Pine Marten are well established and with the spread of the new forests are reported to be on the increase. Wild cat have been sighted as far south as Kielder Forest in Northumberland.

The Polecat is very nearly extinct and will probably go the same way as the beaver and the Wild Boar in the sixteenth century and the Wolf 200 years later.

The thrill of seeing a Golden Eagle will enhance any day on the hills and these birds are more widely distributed than is generally realised. At first a small speck in the sky the eagle will come nearer to satisfy his curiosity. If you are in any doubt about the identity of an eagle you have probably seen a Buzzard which is a much more common and smaller bird of prey, or particularly lower down the glen, a Peregrine Falcon. In Glen Barrisdale on the Knoydart peninsular I have watched a pair of peregrine harry and finally drive off a golden eagle who had ventured into their territory. The golden eagle stands out by its phenomenal size, up to 8 feet wingspan, pronounced neck and beak and feathered legs.

As you climb slowly up from the glen through the heather you may see Red and Black grouse or Golden Plover and then the Ptarmigan which inhabit boulder strewn slopes above 2,000 feet. Ptarmigan change their plumage from brown and grey in summer to white in winter but although they are difficult to pick out against the background their low croaking gives away their position as they scamper to safety.

Other inhabitants of the open inhospitable slopes above 2,000 feet are the Dotterel and the Snow Bunting. The latter are uncommon but on occasions in winter I have put up a flock of these most attractive little birds.

I cannot leave this section without mentioning a species of insect with which any summer visitor to the Highlands will rapidly become acquainted. Culicoides Impunctatus or the biting midge is widespread and at its most abundant between July and September. In the early morning and in the evening the midges swarm and if you react badly to their bites you must take evasive action. To some they are merely a mild irritant but to others they can be a nightmare. They crawl into ears and eyes and up your nose and their bites leave lumps that can last for days. However midges do not like wind and even a light breeze will keep them away. On still evenings my advice is to stay indoors or do up the mouth of your tent securely and if you must venture out cover as much exposed skin as possible. The various chemical insect repellents do work against midges but they need constant reapplication.

The vegetation ot the Highlands is rich in varities of grasses, sedges and rushes which are of interest chiefly to the botanist. A few mountains however do carry spectacular assemblages, their high corries being festooned with alpines just like a natural rock garden.

The most famous of these are the mica-schist mountains of central Perthshire, Ben Lawers in particular. This mountain and the surrounding hills are a National Nature Reserve where collecting is forbidden but an exploration of the cliffs and gullies above 3,000 feet should reveal the beautiful snow gentian, alpine forget-me-not, alpine speedwell, cushions of the pink moss campion and rare saxifrages. In addition the lower meadows are bright with orchids and mountain pansies.

The exposed stone littered Cairngorm plateau is of great interest to the botanist for it is the nearest we have in Britain to arctic tundra. These acid soils bear a cover of lichens, mosses, rushes and dwarf willow. The latter (salix herbacea) is the smallest tree in Britain. It forms a low mat over the gravelly soil with trunks no thicker than matchsticks and a height of less than an inch.

ACCESS

There is no law of trespass in Scotland and provided you keep the country code you may walk anywhere in the mountains.

Certain areas may be restricted in the stalking season, August 9th to October 20th, and during the grouse shooting season, August 12th to December 9th. Always check locally before venturing into the hills during these periods; the estate factors will tell you which hills are being worked on which days. The letting of sporting rights may well be the principal source of income from many of the large Highland estates and the landowners' wishes must be respected.

Private roads run up many glens and permission to drive along these can usually be obtained. I have always found the Forestry Commission very co-operative in this respect and a short drive can bring otherwise remote mountains well within reach.

In the 19th century when labour was cheap the estates employed men on the construction of good paths for ponies to use in bringing down the deer at the end of a day's stalking. Many of these paths still exist and bear witness to the high standards of construction. They are built on stone foundations, are thoroughly drained and paved in places and provide easy access up into the hills.

If you have to climb a deer fence be sure to do so at one of the massive corner posts otherwise the wires can be damaged. These fences are vital to protect young trees from the ravages of deer.

ACCOMMODATION

In the remote areas of the Highlands accommodation is sparse although in the summer many of the cottages and crofts offer bed, breakfast and evening meal. There is a good network of Youth Hostels many of which are splendidly situated among the hills.

The fishing hotels are excellent and cater for the walker and climber as well as for the angler. You can pick up valuable local information from these hotels and the hospitality they offer is in the best Scottish tradition. Log fires even in summer, drying rooms, hot water bottles and other comforts are standard and the cooking is sophisticated.

Camping gives you the freedom of choice and you will be able to find a suitable site for a lightweight tent almost anywhere. If you have a small tent be sure to buy a flysheet to keep out the rain and a close fitting zipped entrance will help to keep out the midges.

Popular areas such as Loch Morlich in the Cairngorms and Glen Coe have organised sites with proper facilities and these are springing up in many other places. You will need one of these sites if you have a large family tent or caravan and a list of these can be obtained from the

Scottish Tourist Board (for address see page 24).

On your walks through the hills you may pass open cottages or bothies situated in remote glens. Formerly these bothies were used by stalkers but over the years they have gradually fallen into ruin and decay. In 1965 however a voluntary organisation called 'The Mountain Bothies Association' was set up with the object of renovating certain bothies, The M.B.A. has done a magnificent job and although working on a very small budget they have re-roofed and re-floored many bothies, often man-hauling timber, roofing sheets and cement over miles of rough country. The renovated bothies are primitive but weatherproof and are open to all comers, free of charge, at all times. Further information can be obtained from the M.B.A.

EQUIPMENT

Proper equipment is the key to maximum enjoyment and adequate safety. The principal criterion of a piece of equipment is that it should do the job for which it was designed. Moreover for mountaineering the equipment should be as light as possible.

It is common to see parties of walkers, with faces set in grim determination, carrying huge rucksacks along mountain paths. This is admirable if their intention is to use the mountains as a testing ground for their fitness but they cannot get much enjoyment out of their walk nor can they appreciate, with sweat pouring into their eyes, all that the hills have to offer.

Of course a certain minimum amount of equipment must always be carried. In Scotland bad weather can arrive at a moment's notice and you must be prepared for it. Similarly conditions above 3,000 feet are very much more severe than those met with in the glens.

A reasonable compromise must be made in the selection of equipment and occasionally you will be caught out. One night in early June I was on a solo walk over the hills from Dundonnell in Ross-shire to Poolewe when a cold front moved over north west Scotland. Three inches of snow fell during the hours of darkness and I was forced to contend with blizzard conditions and iced rocks. With no ice axe, gloves or scarf I suffered miserably and had to move with extreme caution yet I could never advise a hill walker to be prepared for such conditions in June.

Boots are the first essential and should be of moulded rubber sole or vibram variety. They should be comfortable and large enough to enable two pairs of socks to be worn. Lightweight boots are adequate, provided there is sufficient padding under the sole to protect the foot from sharp rocks and the uppers should be rigid enough to give ankle support. Steer clear of boots designed chiefly for rock climbing because they have a steel plate in the sole for rigidity when standing on tiny foot holds. When walking in these boots there is little give and your heels, constantly riding up and down, will soon blister.

Look after your boots by packing them with newspaper when they get wet after a walking holiday. Dubbin them well before putting them away. It is possible to buy special preparations for waterproofing boots but provided your boots are supple and comfortable you should be satisfied. On a wet day in the mountains your feet will get wet anyway. Wear two pairs of woollen socks and your feet will remain warm even if they are wet. Nylon socks are not satisfactory since they encourage sweating, do not retain heat and, by sticking to the feet when damp, may cause blisters.

Apart from your feet you should take every precaution to stay dry. In summer at low level you will be able to get by with a light anorak or plastic mac but on the high ridges in conditions of heavy wind-driven rain you will need special clothing.

For leg warmth I recommend cavalry twill trousers or cord breeches which have the advantage of bagginess round the knees, useful when going up hill. Light cotton jeans or shorts are not suitable unless the weather is settled fine and you are not planning to go high. A pair of proofed nylon overtrousers should be carried in the rucksack; they only weigh a few ounces.

Above the waist wear a shirt and woollen jersey. Even in summer I wear or carry two jerseys and take more in winter. Walking up hills can make you hot and sweaty but once above the tree-line the conditions can be severe and you must be prepared to meet strong, cold winds.

Lightweight cagoules do not alone provide enough protection. I wear a windproof ventile anorak and carry a large neoprene cagoule which is completely waterproof and can be slipped on in seconds if a storm arrives. The anorak and cagoule should have hoods since much heat is lost through the head if it is left unprotected.

Carry a pair of gloves; snow can fall on the mountain tops in every month of the year and hands can quickly become numb. This could be dangerous as well as uncomfortable as you fumble with zips, the map, compass and rucksack straps and waste vital minutes.

In winter you must be prepared to carry more. Never venture out without an ice axe and wear extra clothes. I can recommend pyjama trousers under your breeches and a string vest. A woollen balaclava helmet, snow gaiters, snow goggles and two pairs of gloves are necessities. Dachstein wool mitts together with proofed over-mitts are about the best combination.

If you are expecting to meet hard snow or ice bring crampons (spikes that strap under the boot) as they can save hours of step cutting.

Your clothing and equipment may be tested in winter even without precipitation. Powder snow underfoot can be whipped into blinding spicules which penetrate everything. At times I have been forced to turn away from the wind and bury my face in my gloved hands until the blast has passed. On occasions like these you are glad for the protection of elasticated cuffs, a close fitting hood and gaiters.

When you are walking in the hills you will need a small rucksack. Get into the habit of carrying your own things in your rucksack even when you are with other walkers. If you do share, the rucksack will be heavy and the straps will probably need adjustment at every swop over. Bad feeling and resentment breaks out as you imagine your turn is the longest and the ground is more difficult than your partner's.

A good rucksack will have an inner section that can be extended if necessary for big loads or to act as an emergency bivvy sack reaching to the waist. The load should be carried as high up the back as possible and be distributed so that the heavy articles are near the spine and hence nearly in line with the body's centre of gravity. A waist band is useful to prevent the sack swinging and throwing you off your balance.

Inside your rucksack you should always carry the following items: Spare clothing, food and emergency rations, first aid kit, torch and bivvy bag. Put the compass, map and a whistle in a pocket of your anorak in case the rucksack gets accidentally left behind or falls over a cliff.

A 'Silva' compass is adequate but make quite sure you know thoroughly how to use it for (a) finding your position on the map from observations of the features around you and (b) plotting a route on the map and translating it to the ground.

When plotting a route remember to allow for the magnetic variation of 7° west of true north.

Extras that I always take are a camera and a small flask of whisky. A camera because the contrast and lighting effects you meet in the hills can be startling. The good photos you take will more than compensate for the disappointing days of cloud and mist.

A nip from a small flask of whisky is a great morale booster when you are cold and wet and what better way is there of celebrating your reaching the summit of a new Munro?

One word of caution here; if you or your partner are really desperately tired and cold you should not take spirits. Alcohol will cause blood to flow to the stomach area rather than to places where it is more needed.

MAPS AND COMPASS WORK

The Ordance Survey Maps scale 1 inch to the mile, 1:63,360, or the new metric maps 1:50,000 give sufficient detail for most expeditions. The whole of Scotland is covered by both series and in addition three special tourist maps of the 1″ scale are available: 'Loch Lomond and The Trossachs', 'The Cairngorms' and Glen Coe and Ben Nevis'.

The half inch to the mile Bartholemews' maps have attractive coloured contouring and enable you to see a wide area without a lot of folding but the scale is too small for accurate route planning.

A scale of 2½ inches to the mile, 1:25,000, is perhaps the optimum. So far the Ordance Survey have issued only two special maps of this scale, 'The Cairngorms' and 'Torridon and the Cuillins' but most other areas are available on their standard sheets.

Taking a Bearing

When in the mountains it is vital to know exactly where you are at all times. This is not very difficult in clear weather but in mist or cloud it can be impossible without a knowledge of compass work. The following account gives in simple terms an explanation of the essentials of route finding in poor visibility.

First get yourself a good compass. The Silva compass which has a transparent base is ideal and satisfactory for quite accurate work.

The points on a compass are measured in degrees and as in school geometry there are 360° in a complete circle. East corresponds to 90° (from north), south to 180° and so on. The advantage of taking a compass bearing in degrees is that far greater accuracy can be obtained. Thus to quote a bearing of 272° is much better than saying just north of west. (Fig. 1) Now the red end of a compass needle points not to true north but to slightly west of north. This difference is called the magnetic variation and it changes according to latitude and the time. In Britain in 1979 it is approximately 8° and it is decreasing by about ½° every six years. (Fig. 2)

Fig. 1

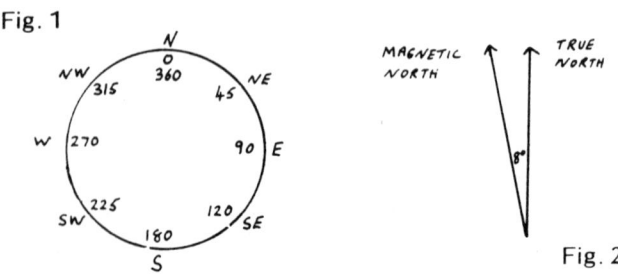

Fig. 2

The grid squares on both the one inch maps and the metric 1:50,000 scale maps represent an area of one square kilometre and the distance between the grid lines represents one kilometre on the ground. These lines do point north and thus, when translating a bearing taken from the map to a bearing you are going to set on the compass, 8° must be added to the map bearing.

Example

Suppose you are standing on the summit of Ben Glas in thick mist and you want to reach the summit of Ben Lawers.

First of all use the compass as a protractor to find the correct bearing from the map. Line up the edge of the compass with the summits of the two mountains and twist the circular surround until the lines etched on the base of the compass are aligned with the north-south grid lines of the map. The bearing in degrees can now be read off the dial where it meets the principal axis of the compass. (Fig. 3). The correct bearing is 43° and note that throughout this operation so far it does not matter in which direction the compass needle is pointing.

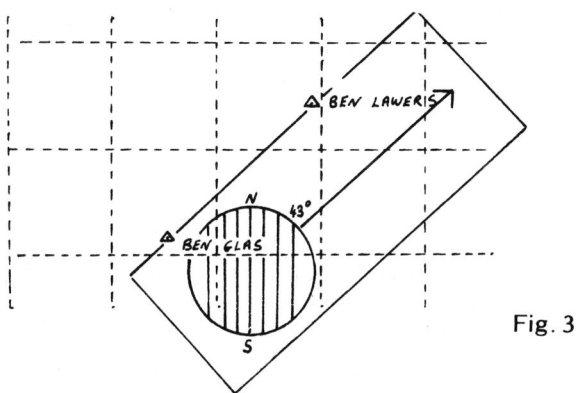

Fig. 3

You can now fold up the map and having added 8° to the map bearing you can march on a magnetic compass bearing of 51° which will lead you to the summit cairn of Ben Lawers.

Rotate the circular dial of your compass until the main

axis corresponds to 51°. Now move the compass round until the red needle points to the N point as indicated on the dial. Walk in the direction of the main axis arrow on the front of the compass and this will be a bearing of 51°.

(Fig. 4)

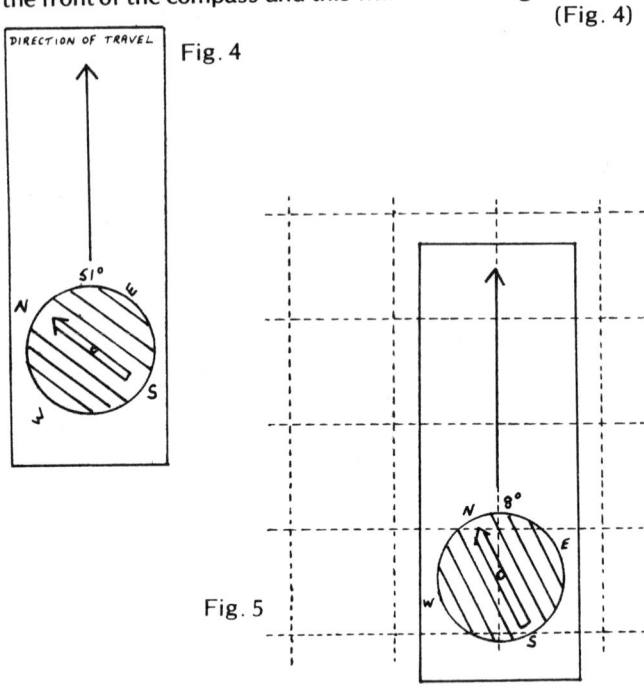

Fig. 4

Fig. 5

Setting the Map

In clear weather features on the landscape can be easily identified by setting the map. This means that when the map is held flat the orientation is such that the actual landscape features are in line with those printed on the map.

Place the map flat on the ground with the compass on top. Rotate the compass dial until it is set at a bearing of 8°. Line up the edge of the compass with a north pointing grid line and then rotate compass and map together until the red needle is aligned with the N mark on the dial. The map is now set. (Fig. 5)

When using a compass be very careful to keep metal objects such as ice picks and zip fasteners well away from the magnetic needle. Certain rocks too can effect the accurate working of the compass, the Cuillin gabbro of Skye being the best known example But in general you must trust the compass. If you go in a different direction governed by your own whim you are sure to be proved wrong.

When walking on a compass bearing keep the needle in sight at all times for it is very easy to stray from the correct bearing particularly when being buffeted by a strong side wind.

Cairngorms

SAFETY FACTORS

Most of the accidents that occur in the hills are caused by ignorance, carelessness or wrong decisions and as such are avoidable.

Bad weather is the principal hazard since conditions can change dramatically. Light rain in the glen can mean blizzard conditions above 3,000 feet since there is a temperature drop of between 3° and 5°F for every 1,000 feet of height.

Here is a list of 20 Do's and Don'ts which you should always adhere to.

1 Leave your route plan and estimated time of your return with a friend or prominently displayed in your car window.

2 Listen to the weather forecast and bear it in mind when planning your route.

3 Don't work on too tight a schedule. Leave time for enjoying the mountain tops and for extra pleasures such as a swim in a stream or loch. Naismith's formula is a useful guide in route planning. Take your speed as 3 m.p.h. and add half an hour for each 1,000 feet of ascent but note this does not allow for halts or bad weather.

4 Double check your equipment before setting out.

5 If you are going more slowly than planned or if a member of the party is feeling unwell make a decision at once and either return or change to a less arduous route.

6 Keep up a good steady pace and don't have too many rests. A stop-go method of progress prevents rhythm and is more exhausting. When walking up hill place the whole of the foot on the ground and not just the toe. Look for level places on which to place the feet.

7 Take plenty of food and remember that light meals at frequent intervals are better than heavy meals at long intervals.

8 Be ready for mist. Use and trust your compass however much you may be convinced you know best. It is sometimes impossible to consult the map in conditions of severe wind and rain and I find it useful to jot down the important features and bearings on a piece of card which I keep in an anorak pocket or a glove.

9 Never underestimate the depth and strength of a stream. In times of spate the smallest streams become raging torrents and may be impassable. It is much better to make a long detour to a bridge or walk upstream until the flow lessens rather than risk being swept away.

10 Never race down scree slopes as you can easily lose control and suffer injury

11 Do not walk alone in the the hills unless you are a very experienced hill walker.

12 Be very careful not to dislodge loose boulders.

13 Don't follow streams downhill as they seldom offer a safe

descent route. You are likely to meet gorges, waterfalls and loose rock.

14 Be as fit as possible. A fit person can extricate himself from a potentially dangerous situation by rapidly moving to easier ground as darkness or bad weather approaches. You will enjoy the hills far more if you are fit as more of your mind can concentrate on the beauty of your surroundings and you will have breath to talk to your friends.

15 If you are walking in a party stay together at all times.

16 Don't attempt any rock climbing unless you know the techniques and have the proper equipment. If when descending you meet cliffs or crumbling rock go back up, traverse round, and try another place.

17 Always carry an ice axe if there is any chance of meeting snow and remember that large patches of snow can last well into summer.

18 Be alert for the condition known as exposure or hypothermia. This condition is potentially very dangerous and it can occur when a walker is thoroughly chilled and exhausted. The symptoms include lethargy, shivering, numbness, pins and needles, and irrational behaviour. Act at once. Put on extra windproof clothing to prevent further heat loss and if possible descend immediately to the glen where conditions are always better. If the symptoms are advanced the patient should not be moved but should be made as comfortable as possible in a sheltered place. Place him in a polythene bivvy bag and if necessary build a small rock wall as windbreak then go immediately for help. If there are more than two in the party leave one member behind with the patient. It is a good idea for the companion to take off his outer clothing and get into the bivvy bag with the patient to provide body warmth. Take some bearings on prominent features to help the rescue party locate the patient.

19 To summon help use the International Distress Signal— six blasts on a whistle (or torch flashes) followed by a pause of a minute then a repetition of the six blasts. When you reach a telephone dial 999 and ask for the Police who have responsibility for co-ordinating the mountain rescue services.

20 Mountain walking in winter brings great rewards. The hills seem vastly higher under their pure white coating

of snow. Your boots crunch through untouched drifts and ice sparkles on the rocks. There is a feeling of intense solitude. In winter, however, there are additional hazards.

(a)   Cornices or lips of snow overhang many ridges and cliff edges. Keep well back.

(b)   Never glissade (slide down snow) unless you can see a gentle run out at the bottom. Always use an ice axe and remain in control.

(c)   Darkness comes early and soft snow or the necessity to cut steps could cause unexpected delays. Be extra careful that you are not be-nighted.

(d)   A sudden drop in temperature after rain can cause rocks to become verglassed and treacherous.

(e)   Avoid steep slopes covered in fresh powder snow, they could avalanche.

USEFUL ADDRESSES

1   The Scottish Tourist Board,
    23 Ravelston Terrace,
    Edinburgh EH4 3EV.

2   Registers of Accommodation, Camping and Caravan Sites,
    Tourism Division,
    Highland and Islands Development Board,
    P.O. Box 7,
    Iverness.

3   Island Ferry Services,
    MacBraynes Ltd.,
    302 Buchanan Street,
    Glasgow G2 3NP.

4   The Nature Conservancy,
    12 Hope Terrace,
    Edinburgh EH9 2AS.

5   Scottish Youth Hostels Association,
    7 Glebe Crescent,
    Stirling.

6   Climbing Courses at Glenmore Lodge, Aviemore.
    Scottish Sports Council,
    4 Queensferry Street,
    Edinburgh.

7   Glencoe School of Winter Climbing,
     Tigdearg, Glencoe,
     Argyll.

8   Hamish Brown Expedition Courses,
     21 Carlin Craig,
     Kinghorn, Fife.

9   John Ridgeway Adventure School,
     Ardmore,
     Sutherland.

10   The Mountain Bothies Association,
     c/o Ian Mitchell,
     40 Maitland Street,
     Dunfermline, Fife.

11   E. Stanford Ltd (Map Suppliers),
     12-14 Long Acre,
     London W.C. 2.

For detailed information on the hills of Scotland you should refer to the guides published by the Scottish Mountaineering Trust. Seven volumes are available dealing with the Southern Highlands, Central Highlands, Western Highlands, Northern Highlands, Islands of Scotland, Island of Skye and the Cairngorms.

If you are interested in learning about rock climbing, or snow and ice climbing you could read *Mountaineering: From Hill Walking to Alpine Climbing* by Alan Blackshaw published by Penguin Books. This excellent book also covers the use of map and compass.

The best way to learn more advanced skills is to go on a course run by an Outdoor Activity Centre or Climbing School. Here you will be taught by qualified instructors and will undertake rock climbing or snow climbing routes led by experts.

For armchair reading I would recommend W. H. Murray's classic *Mountaineering in Scotland* published by Dent. Murray is a fine writer and climber and a great romantic. His infectious enthusiasm for the Highlands stands out on every page and his book provides a pointer to the adventures awaiting you as an aspiring Scottish mountaineer.

FURTHER CHALLENGES

It was no mere chance, that a Scotsman, Dougal Haston, was the first man to scale the south-west face of Everest. Haston served his apprenticeship on the Scottish mountains which can provide climbs as tough as any in the world although on a smaller scale.

The 2,000 foot high vertical north face of Ben Nevis provides routes of the highest standard and in winter the conditions can be more arctic than alpine.

Skye contains 12 mountains of Munro status, all of stark rock, and is a rock climbers' paradise. Thus as well as providing magnificent climbs as ends in themselves Scotland is a training ground for the Alpine and Himalayan climber.

SOME RECOMMENDED EXPEDITIONS
(Map references date to the O.S. 1:50,000 series)

1.   *Suilven* O.S. Sheet 15 Map Ref. 153183
     Time 6-7 hours.

The most dramatic mountain scenery on the mainland of Britain is undoubtedly that of the Assynt area in North west Scotland. Spectacular wedges of sandstone rise steeply from a base of grey Lewisian Gneiss to produce such peaks as Stac Polly, Suilven, Canisp, Quinag, Cul Mor and Ben More Coigach. Of these Suilven which towers over the west coast fishing village of Lochinver gets my vote for sheer dramatic impact.

Suilven is not an easily accessible mountain for it is guarded on all sides by lochans which nestle in the dips and scoops of the impervious base rock. Lying east to west as a high ridge with steep sides the only easy route is via a bealach in the ridge which can be reached from either side by a rough scramble.

From Lochinver drive inland to the perfectly situated Glencanisp Lodge. This beautiful house and well-kept garden overlook Loch Druim Suardulain and from it the sheer western end of Suilven called Caisteal Liath (the Grey Castle) looks most forbidding.

The path goes through the rhododendrons to the rear of the house and continues across the foothills, passing a ruined cottage at Suileag, to Loch na Gainimh, a distance of 4½ miles. Leave the main path just before the western end of the loch and make your way across the lower slopes of Suilven towards the obvious bealach on the ridge. At this point you are only a mile away from the main massif of Suilven and the steep gully leading to the bealach can easily be seen.

Once in the gully it is a 700 ft climb over scree and loose rocks to the broad main ridge. The summit of Suilven is the top of Caisteal Liath a short distance away to the west. It is an easy walk, mainly over grass.

At the highest point, 2399 ft, there is a small cairn and a large flat boulder which makes an ideal spot for lunch. In clear weather you will be able to see from An Teallach in the south to Foinaven and Arkle in the north and much of the western seaboard in between. You may be tempted to linger on the summit for hours on a warm summer evening but remember you are far from home.

Return to the bealach on the ridge and descend the scree gully to regain the path by Loch na Gainimh.

An alternative route, if transport can be arranged, is to descend south from the bealach, also down a scree gully, to reach the moorland beside Fionn Loch. This is a desolate and remote region but a narrow path is met which leads west to the river Kirkaig. If you do descend by this route it is well worth making the five minute detour from the path to see the Kirkaig Falls which are most spectacular and where I have often watched salmon leaping.

The walk to the Falls from the road at Inver Kirkaig is popular with tourists and the path is very clearly marked.

Stac Polly

2. *Stac Polly* O.S. Sheet 15. Map Ref. 106105
    Time 4 hours.

This attractive spiky ridged mountain in the north west gives some simple rock scrambling and magnificent views of the spectacular Ross-shire and Sutherland hills and coast line.

Leave the Nature Reserve car park beside Loch Lurgain and follow the well marked path steeply up to the main ridge. The summit lies at the western end and you can either scramble along the crest of the sandstone ridge or take a narrow path on the north side. Return down the north facing scree slope and traverse round the eastern shoulder to regain the road. There is a path all the way; given clear weather you will have marvellous views of Cul Mor, Suilven and Canisp.

3. *Beinn Dearg* O.S. Sheet 20. Map Ref. 259812
   Time 7 hours.

Beinn Dearg is the highest mountain in a remote group of Munros west of the Garve—Ullapool road and north of the Loch Glascarnoch reservoir. Seen from Ullapool, Beinn Dearg appears as a long whale-back but from the east its buttresses and rock ridges look very fine. In order to make a circular but not too demanding walk I have included two neighbouring Munros along with the ascent of Beinn Dearg.

Start at the telephone box beside Inverlael Lodge which is situated at the southern end of Loch Broom. Walk along the forestry road past the cottage at Glensguaib and follow the burn until you emerge from the trees. Continue along the path up Glen Guaib for a further 1½ miles and then make your way east across the heather until you see the attractive lochan set under the cliffs of Eididh nan Clach Geala. Scramble up the rocks on the west side of the lochan and traverse the summit ridge. Eididh nan Clach Geala is your first Munro of the day at 3,039 ft.

Now make your way south, first to the bealach under Meall nan Ceapraichean and then across the flat plateau to the summit cairn at 3,192.

The steep north facing slopes of Beinn Dearg confront you across another bealach where there is a group of tiny lochans. These slopes become precipitous on the west side where huge snow patches linger well into the summer months. The route to the flat top of Beinn Dearg lies to the right of the cliffs up a field of chaotically piled boulders but nowhere is the going difficult.

The view from Beinn Dearg is magnificent. An Teallach and the Torridon peaks away to the south west, the Fannichs close by to the south while to the north the superb sandstone peaks of Ciogach and Assynt stand out clearly. Far out to the west, beyond Ullapool, are the Summer Isles which, when the sea is calm, appear to be floating on air.

An old wall is a useful guide in misty weather for the long descent down the north west ridge. There is no easy way to regain upper Glen Guaib because the north side of the ridge is sheer and it is best to keep your height for at least two miles until heathery slopes lead gently down to the glen one mile east of the Inverlael forestry plantation.

4.   *Sgurr Mor Fannich* O.S. Sheet 20. Map Ref. 203718
     Time 6 hours

The Fannichs are a compact range of mainly grassy hills which lie south of the A835 Garve—Ullapool road in Ross-shire. The range comprises nine Munros the highest of which is the spectacular fang of Sgurr Mor at 3,637 ft, a mountain which is not overlooked by any other further north in Britain.

The Fannichs make for delightful walking at any season whether it is over cropped turf in the summer or crisp snow in the winter. The hillsides are open and the ridges are broad and obvious, making route finding, even in mist, a relatively easy task.

The best access to the Fannichs is from the A835 which runs along the north side of the range over the pass called the Dirrie More. Leave the road one mile west of Loch Droma and follow the path alongside the Allt a' Mhadadh. After one mile strike south up the north shoulder of Beinn Liath Mhor and after a 1,700 ft climb you will arrive on its summit plateau at 3,120 ft. The summit plateau of Beinn Liath Mhor is covered with flat grey stones hence its name the High Grey Mountain.

Sgurr Mor lies only one mile away to the west and the ridge descends 200 ft to a bealach before swinging round to the north and climbing steeply to its pointed summit. There is a large and well constructed cairn on Sgurr Mor set on the edge of the east face which although not quite sheer is extremely steep and impressive. The view is quite as good as that from neighbouring Beinn Dearg particularly west down Loch Broom and the mountains of Harris in the Outer Hebrides are visible on a clear day.

Descend the ridge northwards and traverse round the head of Coire Mhoir on the east side of which you will see the triangular shaped rock buttress, split with cracks and gullies, of Sgurr nan Clach Geala. This is the finest rock face in the Fannich range.

Continue walking north west and climb to the flat top of Meall a' Chrasgaidh, your third Munro of the day. Descend the long north east ridge which overlooks Loch a' Mhadaidh and thereby reach the peat hagged lower slopes of Creag Raineach Mor. Keep bearing east and you will soon meet the good track beside the Allt a' Mhadadh which leads to the main road back at your starting point.

5. *An Teallach* O.S. Sheet 19. Map ref. 068844
   Time 8-9 hours.

This is a long expedition in wild and rugged country but An Teallach will give you an unforgettable day's mountaineering and it is one of my favourite peaks in all Scotland.

Leave the A832 about half a mile south of Dundonnell House and follow the rough pony track that leads to Achneigie. From the highest point on this track strike north west across the heather to the broad flank of Sail Liath. Climb Sail Liath to reach the beginning of the switchback ridge that leads in 2 miles to Bidein a' Ghlas Thuill, at 3,484 feet the highest point of An Teallach. The ridge is rocky and can give some exhilarating scrambling, particularly over the rock tooth known as Lord Berkeley's Seat. The slopes fall steeply away to the west while to the east 1,500 foot cliffs drop into a coire loch. For the less adventurous a small path by-passes the rocky crest of the ridge.

Descend north from Bidein a' Ghlas Thuill for half a mile and then follow the ridge round in a north easterly direction to reach Glas Mheal for the last nail in the horseshoe. Pick your way carefully down the boulder strewn slopes to the rough glen leading to Dundonnell Hotel for your well-earned glass of beer.

6. *Slioch* O.S. Sheet 19. Map Ref 005689.
   Time 6-7 hours.

Loch Maree more than any other Scottish loch has

retained its character throughout the centuries. Along its shores have survived stands of the old original forest of Scots pine and silver birch and mercifully the loch has escaped the ravages of the Hydro Electric Board. Dominating the eastern end of Loch Maree is the mountain of Slioch which rises to a height of 3,217 ft and throws down cliffs and rock buttresses to the west.

The shortest route to the summit of Slioch is from Letterewe on the north side of Loch Maree but there is no road to Letterewe and boats are difficult to hire from across the water at the Loch Maree Hotel. A slightly longer but equally pleasant route is from Kinlochewe.

Cross the Kinlochewe river by the bridge 500m east of the Kinlochewe Hotel and take the path across the fields which after a mile rejoins the river on its north bank. The path meanders through scattered and decayed birch trees until it reaches the edge of Loch Maree. Shortly afterwards you will arrive at Glen Bianasdail down which foams a considerable burn. Cross this burn by a narrow bridge which spans a picturesque gorge and climb up into the glen by a narrow path. I was once lucky enough to see, quite close at hand, the herd of wild goats which inhabit this region. They were black and white with shaggy hair and had long curved horns.

Slioch and its satellite peaks make up a vast horseshoe surrounding Coire na Sleaghaich on the west side of Glen Bianasdail. There is no path up into the horseshoe but the burn draining the coire cascades down into Glen Bianasdail and if you follow it you cannot go wrong. As you surmount the lip of the coire it opens out into a wide amphitheatre and the floor is littered with huge boulders.

The slopes of the southernmost peak of the horseshoe, Meall Each, are precipitous but if you walk further into the coire you can easily scramble up to the main south east ridge of Slioch. Just before the final slopes you will pass a tiny lochan on the sandstone ridge. The summit trig of Slioch is set on the edge of the plateau overlooking the south facing cliffs.

Walk round to the eastern summit, Sgurr an Tuill Bhain, which is only one mile away along a broad ridge. From there it is an easy descent down into Coire na Sleaghaich and thence to Glen Bianasdail.

An alternative route to Kinlochewe, although four miles longer, is to continue climbing north up Glen Bianasdail until you reach the east end of Lochan Fada. Lochan Fada is a dark and gloomy but magnificent stretch of water four miles long set amidst high and rocky mountains. Cross the river by stepping stones and walk across the shore at the end of the lochan until you meet the good stalkers' track running through Gleann na Muic. Follow this south through the group of cottages known as the Heights of Kinlochewe until you are back at your starting point.

West from Coire Mhic Fhearchair

7. *Ben Eighe* O.S. Sheet 19. Map Ref. 951511
   Time 8-9 hours.

Ben Eighe is one of the quartzite capped giants of the Torridon range. It forms a 4 mile long ridge that is narrow and exciting in places and on the west side there is a coire that ranks as one of Scotland's most dramatic.

Start from the car park near the road bridge four miles up Glen Torridon from the loch. A good path leads up Coire Dubh under the east buttress of the equally fine Torridon mountain Liathach. The track becomes less distinct at the watershed but a line of cairns lead you around the shoulder of Sail Mhor. Quite suddenly you surmount the lip of Coire Mhic Fhearchair and you stand beside the small loch ringed by the grandest scenery in Scotland. Three huge buttresses fully 1,500 feet high rise into the sky beyond the loch. The buttresses are of glistening white quartzite standing on plinths of red sandstone.

Climb steeply up the scree slopes on the east side of the loch to reach Ruadh-stac Mor, at 3,309 feet the highest summit of Ben Eighe. Now you have gained your height you have a magnificent high level ridge walk ahead of you. First walk south to meet the main ridge then west for three miles over Sgurr Ban and beyond where rock gives way to heather slopes and you descend to the road conveniently near the Kinlochewe Hotel.

Liathach

8. *Liathach* O.S. Sheet 25. Map Ref. 929580
Time 6-7 hours.

Liathach and Beinn Eighe are the giants of Torridon. Beinn Eighe has a more varied and complex structure of cliffs and coires but Liathach rising above Glen Torridon as a monolith of rock has more immediate impact on the traveller driving south from Kinlochewe. Both mountains are quartzite but whereas Beinn Eighe throws down vast scree slopes on the south side which glisten white after rain, the summit ridge of Liathach is poised over rock buttresses and towers and few escape routes can be found. The two mountains are separated by the low pass called the Coire Dubh only 1,200 ft above sea level.

The full traverse of the Liathach ridge is three miles long and it calls for a good head for heights and some scrambling ability although, if desired, the exposed sections can be by-passed by a narrow path running below the apex on the south side.

Start the walk from the car park near the bridge over the Coire Dubh burn four miles east of Torridon village. Since the eastern top of Liathach, Stuc a' Choire Dhuibh Bhig, is precipitous on the Coire Dubh side it is best to ascend a coire on the west side of this top to gain access to the ridge proper.

Walk down the road for a mile and then strike up the steep hiilside where a large burn drains the upper coire. For a few hundred feet there is a rough path but after that you must pick your own route through the rock outcrops and across the boulder fields until you arrive at the bealach on the ridge. The bealach is mid way between the eastern top and the impressive triangular shaped face of Spidean a' Choire Leith 3,456 ft. It is well worthwhile making the short detour eastwards to take in the summit of Stuc a' Choire Dhuibh Bhig for it is a fine view point for the main ridge of Liathach and the surrounding Torridon peaks.

The traverse ahead over Spidean a' Choire Leith to the western summit of Mullach an Rathain is sheer delight. The views of dramatic rock scenery on all sides are scarcely bettered on the mainland of Britain and the going is always interesting and demanding. Beyond Spidean a' Choire Leith the ridge narrows to a razor edge at the famous Pinnacles of Am Fasarinen. The drop on the north side is sheer and the exposure is high but the difficulties are short lived and can be avoided altogether by the detour path 100 ft below.

After the Pinnacles the ridge broadens out and becomes grassy for a stretch before it climbs again to the boulder strewn summit of Mullach an Rathain. Descend the quartzite slopes west for half a mile and then, on the south side, you will find a scree shoot which can be run right down to the heather just above the Post Office at Torridon village. I have made this descent from Mullach an Rathain in 35 minutes but don't try to beat records, keep control and arrive at Torridon in one piece.

Sgurr nan Ceathreamhnan

9. *Sgurr nan Ceathreamhnan* O.S. Sheets 25 & 33.
Map ref. 057228
Time 8-9 hours.

This beautiful mountain with twin summits rises to a height of 3,771 ft and dominates the west end of Glen Affric. From which ever side you observe Sgurr nan Ceathreamhnan it appears perfectly proportioned with high coires falling away from its shapely summit and although it is topped by neighbouring Mam Soul and Carn Eige it is a superior mountain on every other count.

One mile east of the Cluanie Inn in Kintail a pass, the An Caorunn Mor, runs north through the mountains to Alltbeithe in Glen Affric. Walk through this pass following first a good Land Rover track and then, when this stops, a narrow and wet path which leads down to the river in Glen Affric. It is a tough six mile walk into Glen Affric for the path rises to 1,300 ft at the watershed and it is very boggy.

As you descend to the Affric river you will see the Fionn Glen coming in on the left and the sturdy bothy of

Camban built under the southern slopes of Beinn Fhada. The collection of wooden buildings straight ahead across the river is the Youth Hostel of Alltbeithe. The Y.H. has a resident warden during the summer months and it is left unlocked throughout the winter so it can act as an emergency refuge.

Cross the river by the bridge which is opposite the Y.H. and climb the grassy slopes ahead until you reach the long eastern ridge of Sgurr nan Ceathreamhnan at a height of 2,700 ft. From here to the top of the mountain the route is obvious, just follow the grassy ridge westwards which steepens considerably as you approach the summit.

Coires and ridges fall away on all sides and the summit ridge between the two tops is quite airy. To the west you look out to Loch Duich, Loch Alsh and Skye while to the north you see nothing but range upon range of mountains in one of the remotest areas of the Highlands.

From the western top descend the grassy south ridge for a knee jarring 2,500 ft until you are back in Glen Affric again. Unless you wish to return down the Fionn Glen and Glen Licht to Morvich, a distance of ten miles, there is no alternative but to retrace your footsteps through the An Caorunn Mor to Cluanie.

10.   *Mam Soul* [*Sodhail*] *and Carn Eige* O.S. Sheet 19. Map Ref. 120253.

Time 10 hours.

These two peaks, both over 3,800 feet high, command the three great glens of the western highlands. Possibly the most remote area in all Scotland, glens Affric, Cannich and Strathfarrar drain the hills eastwards to the Beauty Firth.

From Cannich drive west alongside Loch Beinn a' Mheadhoin and park at the locked gate just short of Affric Lodge. Glen Affric is most spectacular with stands of Scots Pine, a roaring river and it is overlooked by high mountains. I have seen capercaillie in the woods beside Loch Affric.

From Affric Lodge climb to the top of Sgurr na Lapaich the prominent peak above the loch. This summit is the end of a 2½ mile long ridge thrown out from Mam Soul and it provides a delightful walk. Mam Soul is a rounded mountain and being so prominent it was used as a sighting station for one of the early surveys of Scotland. A rough stone shelter was built for the Surveyors and the ruins of this can still be seen not far from the summit.

Drop steeply down to the col below Carn Eige and then climb up again to the summit of this peak which overlooks Mam Soul by 15 feet. Continue eastwards along another ridge that is rocky and narrow in places and in 3 miles this leads to another shapely peak Tom a' Choinich (the mossy peak). Descend steeply on the east side to reach a low col and you will meet a good path leading down the glen to the road beside Loch Beinn a' Mheadhoin.

This is a typically Scottish hill walking expedition, rich in scenery and adventure, and although it makes a long day I can highy recommend it to a fit party.

11. *The Five Sisters of Kintail* O.S. Sheet 33.
    Map Ref. 978166.
    Time 7 hours.

Travellers to Skye will be well acquainted with one of Scotland's best known and most romantic views, that of Eilean Donan Castle set against the background of Loch Duich and the Five Sisters of Kintail.

The Five Sisters are the westernmost peaks of a long ridge of high mountains stretching west from Cluanie in Kintail to Shiel Bridge. The ridge is best traversed from east to west for in that direction you can enjoy the magnificent sea and mountain landscape and you also gain the benefit of starting 600 ft above sea level.

One mile east of the Glenshiel battle site there is a break in the forestry plantation on the north side of the road. Running up through the break there is a narrow path which leads to the low bealach on the main ridge west of Saileag. Take this route to the Five Sisters ridge which now stretches away westwards for six switch-back miles.

The first summit on the ridge is the rock peak of Coirein nan Spainteach which leads to Sgurr na Ciste Duibhe, a shapely mountain with cliffs on the north and east sides.

The ridge now turns north and descends 600 ft before rising to Sgurr na Carnach and Sgurr Fhuaran. At 3,305 ft Sgurr Fhuaran is the principal summit of the Five Sisters ridge and it is a fine mountain from every angle. A steep and rocky coire falls away north from its pointed summit and it commands a superb view. To the west the Cuillin of Skye, to the south the Saddle and Ladhar Bheinn and to the north Beinn Fhada and the peaks of Glen Affric and Torridon.

Descend the steep north ridge keeping to the lip of the coire until the ridge broadens out. Continue north over Sgurr nan Saighead which has a wide north facing coire just below the summit and descend to the plateau of Sgurr na Moraich which at 2,870 ft marks the last of the Five Sisters. Descend the western slopes which are grassy and easy angled to meet the main road one mile north of Shiel Bridge.

12. *Gleouraich and Spidean Mialach* O.S. Sheet 33.
     Map Ref. 040053.
     Time 5-6 hours.

Gleouraich and Spidean Mialach rise above the north banks of Loch Quoich near the eastern borders of Knoydart, a loch which is long and lonesome and seldom visited. Most visitors to Scotland roar through Glen Garry, Cluanie and Kintail on the main road to Skye, ignorant of the narrow cul-de-sac which winds over the hills to Kinloch Hourn.

Three miles after Quoich dam and one mile before Quoich Bridge you pass, on the right of the road, a small and decayed plantation which has been overgrown by rhododendrons. On the west side of this plantation runs a sizeable burn, the Allt Coire Peitireach. At this point an ancient although still well defined stalkers' path starts winding its way up the southern slopes of Gleouraich. It is well worthwhile locating this path because it is a masterpiece of its kind, wide, well contoured and properly drained.

The stalkers' path leads to the main summit ridge of Gleouraich which is rocky and precipitous to the north and in winter is heavily corniced. I have seen Golden Eagles on these cliffs. Looking north from the cairn at 3,395 ft you have an excellent view of the long South Kintail Ridge while to the south and west you can follow the Gairich, Sgurr Mor ridge all the way to the pointed summit of Sgurr na Ciche. In bad weather you can see the squalls of wind and rain approaching down Loch Quoich and whipping up the surface of the loch, a magnificent sight under grey and lowering clouds.

Follow the main ridge east to the bealach, at 2,450 ft, under Spidean Mialach. The ascent of the Spidean is easy but rough and once more the steepest ground is to the north where cliffs fall away dramatically towards upper Glen Loyne. Spidean Mialach is another Munro at a height of 3,268 ft.

The descent of Spidean Mialach is very rapid and easy and almost any line can be taken down the southern slopes to the road at Quoich dam.

13. *Sgurr na Ciche* O.S Sheet 33. Map Ref. 902966
Time 8 hours.

The ascent of Sgurr na Ciche involves a long day's climb across trackless wastes on the border of the Knoydart peninsular. However the mountain is beautifully shaped with a sharp pointed summit which is a superb view point for the Western Highlands, and the expedition is a most rewarding experience. Standing on the summit of Sgurr na Ciche you are as far from civilisation as on almost any other peak in Britain. But it is an expedition for a fit and competent party because there are no easy escape routes and the mountain is exposed to the worst of the westerly gales.

Drive along to the western end of Loch Arkaig and park beside the farmhouse at Strathan. It is possible to continue along the very steep and rough road for another mile to Glendessary House but it is not worth the risk of damaging your car in such an inaccessible spot.

Walk up into Glen Dessary passing the remote cottage of Upper Glendessary from where, looking south across the river, you will be able to see the A' Chuil bothy which has recently been renovated by the Mountain Bothies Association.

Two miles beyond Upper Glendessary the glen divides and at this point a burn rushes down a ravine on the right. Climb up the steep and grassy slopes on the west side of the burn to gain the summit of Sgurr nan Coireachan. It is a pull of nearly 2,500 ft up the relentless slopes. To the north you look down on the western end of Loch Quoich and before the level of the loch was raised by building a dam at the eastern end, thereby flooding the glen, a rain gauge showed Kinlochquoich to be the wettest place in Britain with an average annual rainfall of 159 inches.

Descend the rocky slopes to the west and continue over the switchback ridge to Garbh Chioch Mhor. In misty weather you can follow the remnants of an old fence which keeps to the crest of the ridge. There is a tiny lochan on the bealach under Sgurr na Ciche and the rocks ahead look very steep and forbidding. The best route from the bealach to the pointed summit of Sgurr na Ciche is to traverse round to the south side and then work your way up through the broken cliffs. The summit is truly sharp, there is barely room for the trig point at 3410 ft, but it is a fine view point for Morar, Loch Nevis, Loch Hourn and the Kintail hills.

Return to the bealach and scramble down the steep and narrow gully on the south side which surprisingly quickly leads you down to grassy slopes above Lochan a' Mhaim. As you descend from the bealach keep working round south and east because if you follow the natural lie of the land you will end up at the ruined cottage of Finiskaig beside Loch Nevis.

From Lochan a' Mhaim it is a pleasant seven mile walk back through Glen Dessary to your car at Strathan.

14. *Ladhar Bheinn* O.S. Sheet 33. Map Ref. 825040.
Time 9-10 hours.

Ladhar Bheinn in Knoydart offers the perfect combination of grandeur and remoteness and being situated on a peninsular the sea is ever present.

The quickest way to reach the base of the mountain would be to cross Loch Hourn from Arnisdale to Barrisdale bay but there is no regular motor boat service and the longer route from Kinlochhourn is more sure. The coastal hamlet of Kinlochhourn marks the end of the road through Glen Garry which passes Tomdoun and Loch Quoich.

The walk over Ladhar Bheinn can either start and finish at Kinlochhourn or it can finish at Inverie on the south side of the Knoydart peninsular. Make your choice and arrange transport accordingly.

From the jetty at Linlochhourn walk along the south side

of the loch following a narrow switchback path which passes two cottages, Skiary and Runival, on its way to Barrisdale bay. Loch Hourn is a gloomy and sombre loch situated in a deep and narrow defile and more than any other in scotland it resembles a Norwegian fjord. The only scar on the landscape is the power line which marches across the hills on the north side of the loch on its way to the Isle of Skye.

At Barrisdale the loch opens out and you may see cattle grazing the shore outside Barrisdale House. As you round the corner into Glen Barrisdale the stupendous peak of Ladhar Bheinn comes into view rising 3,343 ft from sea level in a complex of cliffs and corries.

Cross the Barrisdale river by the bridge and follow the old stalkers' path up into Coire Dhorrcail. Cliffs seal off the head of this dramatic coire but on the north side you can reach the ridge of Druim a' Coire Odhair by a steep ascent over rough grass. Follow this fine ridge to the summit cairn of Ladhar Bheinn and pause to admire the magnificent views both inland to the pointed summit of Sgurr na Ciche and west across the Sound of Sleat to the Cuillin of Skye.

Continue along the narrow summit ridge in the south easterly direction until you reach the bealach under Aonach Sgoilte, climb this subsidiary peak and then descend sharply to the Inverie track where it crosses the watershed at Mam Barrisdale.

Now from this point you can either return back down the track to Glen Barrisdale and Kinlochhourn or you can proceed south down Gleann an Dubh Lochain to Inverie, a walk of six miles. From Inverie you can catch a ferry boat across Loch Nevis to Mallaig and this makes a fitting end to the walk. But if you do decide to walk across Knoydart to Inverie be sure to check first the times of the (infrequent) ferry or arrange with a boatman in Mallaig to be collected at Inverie. There is a public telephone box at Inverie but otherwise there are no facilities or accommodation available and the estate is private.

15.   *Sgurr Alasdair* O.S. Sheet 32. Map Ref. 450208.
Time 6 hours.

The Cuillin of Skye offer the most dramatic mountain

scenery in the British Isles. The peaks are composed of black volcanic rock called gabbro which has been weathered into fantastic ridges and pinnacles. Gabbro is a sound and rough rock which gives excellent grip for the climber and the Cuillin provide an unlimited number of rock routes of all standards and types.

Unless you have some experience of rock climbing you should not venture out alone to explore the Cuillin. Even the famous Cuillin Ridge which rises straight out of the sea and encloses the lochs of Coruisk and Scavaig contains several pitches of real climbing.

However the walker can still experience the unique scenery of the wild rocky coires, precipices and razor ridges by selecting his routes carefully. A walker with a good head for heights and some scrambling ability can climb many of the mountains including the sharp pinnacle of Sgurr Alasdair, at 3,251 ft the highest peak in Skye.

A few points of warning before you set out for Sgurr Alasdair. You must wear proper leather climbing boots for there is little grass or vegetation on the upper slopes of the Cuillin and much of the going is over rough boulders and scree. Choose fine weather for your walk because on a clear day the views and opportunities for photography are unsurpassed, besides which you must not risk losing your way in mist for the gabbro rock is magnetic and compasses cannot be fully trusted.

Start from the village of Glen Brittle which is at the road end on the west side of the Cuillin. Two rather boggy paths lead up the hillside from the Glen Brittle Memorial Hut, one makes for the spectacular waterfall and gorge in Glen Banachdich while the other follows a traverse line into Coire Lagan. Take the latter path which climbs to the Loch-an-Fhir-bhallaich under the steep west ridge of Sgurr Dearg. The translation 'Loch of the Brown Trout' is apt for I have camped on its banks and caught trout for my supper every night.

Ascend the rough slopes right up into the bowl of Coire Lagan, cross a wide area of flat boiler plate slabs and pause beside Loch Lagan. You are surrounded by many of the Cuillin giants arranged in a horseshoe, from left to right, Sgurr Dearg, An Stac, Sgurr Mhic Choinnich, Sgurr Alasdair and Sgurr Sgumain. The vast face of rock below Sugmain is Sron na Ciche, the most famous of all the Cuillin cliffs for rock climbing.

The lower slopes of Sgurr Alasdair make up a giant fan shaped slope of scree which narrows to a gully higher up and leads to a bealach on the east side of the mountain. This is the Alasdair Stone Shoot and it provides a simple but laborious way to the summit.

Low down on the shoot the boulders are large enough for you to stand on securely but the higher you climb the smaller and less stable they become. It is an exhausting and frustrating ascent but when you meet the ridge at the top you are rewarded by a magnificent view of the Dubh ridge and the upper Coruisk basin. The summit of Sgurr Alasdair lies up the sharp ridge on the right and it is indeed a true pinnacle with awesome drops on every side. The entire Cuillin ridge can be see from Gars-Bheinn in the south to Sgurr nan Gillean in the north and the view of the two outlying peaks of Blaven and Clach Glas in the west is particularly fine. Across the Sound of Sleat rise the attractive mountains of the Cuillin of Rhum.

Return to Glen Brittle by the same route for every other way is fraught with dangers for the inexperienced.

16. *Sgurr nan Gillean* O.S. Sheet 32. Map Ref. 472253.
   Time 6 hours.

Sgurr nan Gillean is the first peak of the black Cuillin of Skye which comes into view when driving from the ferry at Kyleakin to Portree. From the Sligachan Hotel the peak looks particularly sharp and enticing to the mountaineer being supported on one side by a number of other jagged pinnacles and on the other side by the jutting out tusk of rock called the Bhasteir Tooth.

From the Sligachan Hotel walk 200 metres along the Carbost road until you see an obvious path coming in on the left. Follow this path as it crosses the Allt Dearg Mor burn by a bridge and then winds its way across the rather peaty heather covered slopes to the south. After a mile you come to another big burn, the Allt Dearg Beag, and you should follow its banks for a short stretch until the path divides. The right hand branch leads up into Coire a' Bhasteir and the left hand branch, which you must take, climbs up to Coire Riabhach. This path is well cairned and

Blaven from Sgurr nan Gillean

it traverses the head of Coire Riabhach well above the coire loch and then crosses the rocky lower slopes of the famous Pinnacle Ridge of Sgurr nan Gillean.

The path then swings round to the west and climbs steeply up a long scree slope to gain the crest of the south east ridge of Sgurr nan Gillean. The summit lies to the north and the ridge is interesting and exposed but no real difficulties are experienced. The actual summit is a tiny platform of rock poised over the deep abyss of Lota Coire and it provides an eagle's view of the Cuillin and the mainland mountains of the Western Highlands. Across Glen Sligachan are Marsco, Glamaig and other mountains of the Red Cuillin; these mountains are not built of gabbro but of crumbly pink granite.

Sgurr nan Gillean is one of the most famous peaks anywhere in the world; it is a mountaineer's peak and I always feel moved when, standing on the summit pinnacle, I think of the great climbers who have stood there before me.

Unless you are an experienced climber you must return to Sligachan the same way. But for the rock climber there is an alternative route which entails the descent of the west ridge to Bealach a' Bhasteir and then a rough

45

scramble down Coire a' Bhasteir to regain the path beside the Allt Dearg Beag. The west ridge of Sgurr nan Gillean is straightforward for most of the way until you suddenly find the ridge blocked by an overhanging rock pinnacle called a 'gendarme' or 'policeman'. It is the negotiation of this 'gendarme' which calls for some elementary rock climbing ability. The 'gendarme' is traversed just below the top on the north side, only two or three moves are necessary but it is in an exposed position.

I can thoroughly recommend the ascent of Sgurr nan Gillean, for nobody can claim a knowledge of the Scottish Highlands unless they have climbed in the unique Cuillin range.

Rhum from Sgarr Dearg

17. *The Mountains of Rhum* O.S. Sheet 39.
Time 8 or 11 hours.

The Isle of Rhum is the jewel of the Inner Hebrides and I have yet to meet a climber who has sampled its magic and is not completely under its spell. Completely unspoilt (it is a Nature Reserve) Rhum contains a small range of volcanic rock peaks and with the waves pounding the rugged coastline you are ever conscious of the sea.

A Macbraynes steamer from Mallaig calls at the island several times a week but if you wish to stay for more than a day you must obtain prior permission from the Nature Conservancy. There is no accommodation for visitors so you must either camp or walk to a remote bothy at Dibidil 5 miles south of the landing place at Kinloch. When on Rhum you must take special care not to disturb the environment for the island is used for experiments in forestry and the ranching of red deer.

From Kinloch Castle follow the road west for a mile and then strike across rough hillside and climb Barkeval. This summit gives a good view of the peaks still to come as well as the island spread out below and the three other islands, Eigg, Muck and Canna. Across the Sound of Sleat rise the Black Cuillin of Skye.

From Barkeval continue on over Hallival, Askival and Trollaval. These names are of Norse origin and were landmarks to passing ships. The north ridge of Askival gives a sporting scramble but is not difficult and the traverse of the four peaks is sheer delight. On Hallival you will notice many holes or burrows in the ridge; these are the breeding places of vast colonies of Manx Shearwaters.

When you have gained the summit of Trollaval you must make a decision. You can either return to the Bealach an Oir on the east side or you can continue over the final three peaks of the range, Ainshval, Sgurr nan Gillean and Ruinsival. If you decide on the former, continue your descent to Dibidil, one of the most lonesome and secluded bays in all Scotland, and take the coast path back to Kinloch. For the complete traverse descend from Trollaval to the Bealach an Fhuarain and then scramble steeply up Ainshval hence gaining access to the broad ridge leading south to Sgurr nan Gillean. Now retrace your footsteps for half a mile and swing north west to reach Ruinsival.

Although tired by now you must find a way northwards through rock outcrops down to sea level. At Harris where there is an old Mausoleum you meet a good track that leads in 7 miles to Kinloch.

This greater traverse provides one of Scotland's very best mountaineering days but your party must be fit and you should choose spring or summer to get long hours of daylight.

Lochnagar

18. *Lochnagar* O.S. Sheet 44. Map Ref. 243861
    Time 6-7 hours.
    Lochnagar, the principal mountain of the eastern
Cairngorms, is rich in history and romance. Byron wrote
about it and being situated in the Balmoral Forest it has
been ascended by Royalty.
    The mountain has a spectacular mile-long line of north
facing cliffs above a dark lochan and in winter these
provide snow and ice climbs second only in severity to the
north face of Ben Nevis.
    From Ballater drive down Glen Muick to the farm at the
end of Loch Muick. Cross the river by a footbridge and
take the path that winds westwards up the hill and leads to
the col between Meikle Pap and the main bulk of Lochnagar. This col is an excellent view point for the cliffs.
    Skirt the top of the Lochnagar cliffs and walk on north-
wards to gain the summit cairn perched on huge blocks of
rock. The views are extensive; on a clear day Ben Nevis
can be seen beyond the Cairngorms and far to the south
Arthur's Seat in Edinburgh and even the Cheviots in
England have been identified.
    South of Lochnagar summit lies a high barren wasteland
known as the White Mounth. If you walk over this you can

reach, by a sharp descent, the west end of Loch Muick at Glas allt Shiel. This scheduled lodge was built in 1868 by Queen Victoria as a retreat. A good track will now take you alongside Loch Muick and back to your starting point.

19. *Beinn a' Bhuird and Ben Avon* O.S. Sheet 36 & 43
Time 12 hours.   Map Ref. 092006.

The main Cairngorm range throws out an arm to the west which extends north of Braemar to Cock Bridge on the Balmoral—Grantown road. This arm contains the huge flat topped mountains of Beinn a' Bhuird and Ben Avon.

Although these mountains approach the 4,400 ft mark they are neglected by the average walker and skier on account of their remoteness. For the hill walker they provide a long and challenging round which is tremendously rewarding. Beinn a' Bhuird in particular has many grand corries which rival the best anywhere in Scotland and many new routes await the attention of the rock and ice climber.

The mountains carry much snow which lingers on into the summer and perhaps the best time of the year to attempt this walk is late spring when the days are long and warm yet the corries are still ringed with cornices and the burns are alive with melt water.

Start from the car park just beyond the Linn of Dee and walk up the rough road along Glen Lui towards Derry Lodge. Soon after crossing the river you pass a stand of mature Caledonian Pines on the right hand side of the road. Immediately afterwards turn off right along a narrow path which leads over the hills into Glen Quoich. This path goes through a deep defile and passes several small lochans before meeting the Glen Quoich forestry road.

Beinn a' Bhuird and Ben Avon rise ahead above the old forest, a magnificent scene which can hardly have changed for hundreds of years. Follow the road up Glen Quoich for half a mile and then cross the Dubh Ghleann river by a ford. Keep on the road for another mile and then strike north east up steep heather-clad slopes to the south shoulder of Beinn a' Bhuird marked Bruach Mhor on the map.

Eventually you reach the large cairn marking the south top of Beinn a' Bhuird at 3,860 ft and easy walking takes you past three great east facing corries to the main summit two miles further on at a height of 3924 ft.

A short distance ahead lies the edge of the extensive Garbh Coire and you should follow this eastwards passing the rocky summit of Cnap a' Chleirich before descending 700 ft to the bealach, known as the Sneck, under Ben Avon. If you are tired or behind schedule at the Sneck you should leave Ben Avon for another day and return southwards down the long glen which runs into Glen Quoich. There is no shelter or help available near at hand and it is high and dangerous country in which to be benighted.

If you do have time to take in Ben Avon, ascend the slopes of loose granite scree and walk one mile north east to the conspicuous granite tor on which is perched the summit cairn. Ben Avon is characterised by its granite tors which can be seen in many directions protruding from the plateau.

Return to the Sneck and descend the very rough and peaty glen for five long miles until you meet the Glen Quoich path among the trees.

After crossing the ford you can take a different route back. Keep on the Glen Qoich forestry road which leads to the public road near Mar Lodge; it is then only a few miles back to the car park near Linn of Dee.

20.   *Ben Macdui* O.S. Sheet 36. Map Ref. 989990.
      Time 11 hours.

Ben Macdui at 4,300 ft is the second highest mountain in Britain and Queen of the Cairngorms. In spring its melting snows drain to the head waters of the Dee in the east and the Spey in the west, both fine salmon rivers. Lying equidistant from the popular resorts of Aviemore and Braemar its ascent on foot is a long expedition. Probably the quickest way to its summit would be on skis across the plateau from Cairngorm reached by chair lift from the carpark above Coylumbridge. However the pylons and restaurants on Cairngorm are a hateful sight and by far the best way to climb Macdui is from Deeside.

Drive from braemar to the car park just beyond Linn of Dee and walk 4 miles along a rough track to Derry Lodge which is now empty and boarded up. Cross the Derry burn by a footbridge and walk through the ancient and beautiful forest of Derry with its Caledonian pines and herds of deer which come down from the hills in winter for shelter and to feed off the moss.

Keep to the narrow path on the west side of the Derry burn until the path begins its descent to the wide and open section of Glen Derry. At this point strike up the heather covered hillside to gain the broad south ridge of Derry Cairngorm which appears from the ridge as a conspicuous rounded hump carrying a large cairn. Derry Cairngorm at 3,788 ft is a wonderful view point for Ben Macdui and Cairn Toul which is prominent to the west of the Larig Ghru pass.

Descend gently north over boulder strewn slopes and then swing round west keeping to the edge of the steep Coire Sputan Dearg. The last 800 ft is a relentless plod up to the plateau but marker cairns guide you to the summit of Ben Macdui where there is a large cairn and an indicator to help you identify the surrounding peaks.

Leave the summit of Macdui on a compass bearing of 60° and descend gradually for nearly a mile until you meet a path running down towards Loch Etchachan. This beautiful loch is one of the highest in Scotland and it remains frozen until late in the spring. It is surrounded by cliffs on the west side and that is why it is necessary for you to carefully check your direction of approach with the compass.

The exit stream from the loch leads down into Coire Etchachan where you will pass the tiny Hutchinson Memorial Hut nestling under an imposing cliff. From the hut a path leads over an area of peat hags and moraines to Glen Derry.

A new forestry access road is being bulldozed above Glen Derry but you should keep to the lower footpath which leads back to Derry Lodge and thence to your car at Linn of Dee.

I can thoroughly recommend the walk. This rough mountainous country is unsurpassed in Britain, the Cairngorm plateau has arctic vegetation and the glens are rich in wild life.

21.   *Braeriach* O.S. Sheet 36. Map Ref. 953999.
       Time 10 hours.

While Cairngorm itself has been largely destroyed as a mountain of great natural beauty by the advent of the skiing boom, its neighbour, Braeriach, across the Lairig Ghru to the west, is still untouched and unspoilt.

From Aviemore the view of Braeriach lacks distinction and its featureless mass hardly warrants a second glance. But exploration of the extensive high plateau which makes up its summit reveals a complex mountain with magnificent corries on three sides. The Garbh Choire between Braeriach and Cairn Toul has a two mile long sweep of cliffs and is one of the most impressive sights to be seen in Britain. The winters' snows drift deep in the Garbh Choire and snow beds frequently last here throughout the summer.

The walk I recommend approaches Braeriach from the west up Glen Einich, traverses the summit plateau and then descends to the Lairig Ghru path for the return march

From Coylumbridge walk along the private road beside the river through the remmants of the magnificent Rothiemurchus Forest. After two miles you come to the Cairngorm Club footbridge which carries the Lairig Ghru path across the river. Don't cross the river but keep to the west bank and continue walking south until you leave the forest and break out into Glen Einich.

As you walk up Glen Einich and approach the loch, a distance of four miles, the scenery becomes grander and the high ridges on either side, Braeriach to the east and Sgoran Dubh Mor to the West, block out the light. Loch Einich is one of the jewels of the Cairngorms and it is jealously guarded by the Nature Reserve authorities. The gates are securely locked and camping is strictly forbidden. The dark cliffs of Sgoran Dubh are the home of Golden Eagles and in winter they provide high standard snow and ice climbs. Years ago a semaphore was constructed on the summit of Sgoran Dubh Mor to signal the whereabouts of deer to shooting parties down in the glen.

At the north end of Loch Einich, a short way up the hillside to the east, you will see a ruined bothy. From this bothy a path zig-zags up into Coire Dhondail climbing over rocks and boulders in its upper part until it emerges on to the open slopes of Braeriach. From the cliffs of Coire Dhondail to the summit cairn of Braeriach it is a walk of two and a half miles but there is plenty of interest on the way. Keep bearing east until you come to the lip of the great Garbh Choire and follow this round northwards to the Wells of Dee. A stream, the true source of the Dee, bubbles up through the stones and gravel of the Breariach plateau at a height of 4,000 ft. The stream gathers pace and then plunges down into the Garbh Coire.

Cairns built at regular intervals guide you to the summit of Braeriach at 4,248 ft. The summit cairn is poised on the edge of the Coire Bhrochain cliffs and particularly in winter, when huge cornices form, the position is very fine. Perhaps the best view from the summit of Braeriach is south across the Garbh Choire to the Angel's Peak and Cairn Toul. Ben Macdui is close by across the Lairig Ghru but from this side it appears as a massive rounded hump.

Follow the Coire Bhrochain cliffs round to the east for half a mile and then descend north to the broad bealach under Sron na Lairig. From this bealach a path leads down to the Lairig Ghru at a height of 2,733 ft near the Pools of Dee.

It is rough but easy walking down the Lairig path back to Coylumbridge, a distance of eight miles. You pass the Sinclair Memorial Hut, an emergency refuge, built on a moraine above the path and the last few miles are through the sweet smelling pines of Rothiemurchus, a fitting end to a splendid expedition.

22.   *Creag Meagaidh* O.S. Sheet 42. Map Ref. 418875
      Time 6-7 hours.

Creag Meagaidh rises to a height of 3,700 feet north of Glen Spean. The summit plateau carries snow well into the summer and on the east side the slopes fall away to give a stupendous semi-circle of cliffs with a lochan nestling below. This is the famous Coire Ardair, a playground for rock and ice climbers.

Leave the main A68 road at Aberarder beside Loch Laggan and follow the path for 4 miles into Coire Ardair. One warm mid-March day I passed hundreds of lizards basking in the sunshine on the rocks beside this path.

When you reach the lochan you will be able to appreciate the magnificent coire with the cliffs towering 1,400 feet above you. The only line of weakness is the conspicuous gap or window on the north side and this pass was probably used by Bonnie Prince Charlie in 1746. This is the pass you must take to reach the higher slopes of Creag Meagaidh. The slopes are steep but easy and you will soon reach the nearly level summit plateau. The cairn lies one mile west of the top of the coire.

In clear weather you can descend to the glen by a variety of routes but cliffs and coires abound and the safest way is to take the broad ridge running just west of south from the summit. You can follow an old fence for much of the way and pleasant grassy slopes lead to the road at Moy.

Creag Meagaidh, Coire Ardair

23. *Ben Nevis and Carn Mor Dearg* O.S. Sheet 41.
   Map Ref. 167713. Time 8 hours.

Ben Nevis at 4,406 feet is the highest mountain in the British Isles and is a 'must' for the hill walker. Seen from the south or west however it appears; as an unattractive hump, for the stupendous 2,000 foot north face is invisible. For this reason it is worth combining the ascent of

Ben Nevis

Ben Nevis with that of Carn Mor Dearg which lies to the north and provides an excellent view of the face. In addition the two mountains are linked by a narrow and exciting arete. In winter however the descent from Ben Nevis to the Carn Mor Dearg arete should only be attempted by fully equipped and experienced walkers since the slopes are often icy and treacherous.

Cross the river Nevis by the footbridge opposite the Youth Hostel in Glen Nevis and climb steeply up the hillside to meet the pony track that starts from Achintee farm. This pony track leads to the summit of Ben Nevis and the ascent will take between 3 and 4 hours. The track first winds round the shoulder of Meall an Suidhe and then zig-zags up the steep and stony slopes to reach the broad plateau of Nevis. The cliffs lie on the north side and you should keep well away from the edge in winter since enormous cornices form. Near the summit trig point you will see the ruins of an old observatory. The view is superb with mountains and lochs as far as the eye can see and it is possible to pick out distant peaks such as the Cuillin of Skye, the Cairngorms and Ben Lomond.

From the cairn descend the scree slopes in a south

North Face Ben Nevis

easterly direction until you reach a warning notice and a line of posts which will guide you to the arete. In winter conditions of snow or thick mist it is inadvisable to make this descent and you should return to Glen Nevis by the ordinary route.

The arete leads to the summit of Carn Mor Dearg and you can continue north over two subsidiary summits before descending north over two subsidiary summits before descending easy slopes to the main road of the distillery, one mile from Fort William.

24.   *Sgurr a' Mhaim and the Mamores* O.S. Sheet 41.
      Map Ref. 164667. Time 8-9 hours.

Sgurr a' Mhaim is the beautiful and graceful mountain which fills the southern end of Glen Nevis and is so conspicuous in the spring with its high coire filled with snow. It is one of the principal peaks of the Mamore Forest range which is situated between Loch Leven and Glen Nevis. The Mamores are characterised by shapely peaks joined by narrow ridges and they make for ideal hill walking. You can wander at will amongst the hills doing as much or as little as you please for there are many easy escape routes down to Upper Glen Nevis when you are tired.

The walk I recommend starts with the ascent of Sgurr a Mhaim and then follows the main ridge of the Mamores west over three more Munros to Binnein Mor, at 3,700 ft the highest peak in the range.

From the car park at the head of Glen Nevis cross the river by the bridge near the waterfull and make directly for the north west ridge of Sgurr a' Mhaim. There is no path and the grassy slopes are tremendously steep and tiring, the ascent is fully 3,300 ft. Take heart though, for once you have gained the summit ridge of Sgurr a' Mhaim the rest of the day is sheer delight.

Sgurr a' Mhaim is perfectly situated between the major mountain ranges of Nevis, the Aonachs and the Grey Coires to the north and Glen Coe and Lorn to the south. All can be seen in a panoramic view. The true shape of Ben Nevis is evident with the 2,000 ft north face plunging down in silhouette and the gentle convex slopes, up which winds the tourist path, on the west side. The spectacular cascade visible on the slopes of Nevis directly opposite Sgurr a' Mhaim is the famous waterslide of the Allt Coire Eoghainn.

The ridge running south from the summit of Sgurr a' Mhaim to Sgor an Iubhair is known as the Devil's Ridge. It is narrow and exposed, particularly on the east side, but unless under full winter conditions it is not difficult. At Sgor an Iubhair you meet the main backbone of the Mamores and you should follow it east over the summits of Am Bodach 3,382 ft, Stob Coire a' Chairn 3,129 ft, Na Gruagaichean 3,442 ft and then north to Binnein Mor 3,700 ft. The ridge is mainly broad and easy going and the final summit of Binnein Mor, a great triangular wedge, beckons as you approach it from the west.

Descend the steep north west ridge of Binnein Mor which leads down to Upper Glen Nevis. In dry weather you should be able to ford the river easily and reach the good path on the north side but if in doubt keep to the south side until you come to the suspension bridge near the waterfall and climbers' hut at Steall.

The path now descends the Nevis Gorge beside the river cascading down its rocky bed in a fury while the setting of Oaks, Birch and Scots Pine is magnificent.

A few years ago plans were mooted to dam this gorge

Sgurr A' Mhaim

and flood Upper Glen Nevis for a hydro-electric scheme but thankfully they have now been abandoned.

25. *Ben Alder* O.S. Sheet 42. Map Ref. 496719.
     Time: A 2-day Expedition.
     This huge and remote mountain dominates the vast tract of country between the railway line over Rannoch Moor and the village of Dalwhinnie on the A9 Perth—Inverness road. Although it rises to a height of 3,757 ft it can barely be seen by the unadventurous traveller; a glimpse of its snow covered flanks away north of Loch Ericht on a clear winter's day from Dalwhinnie is all that is possible.
     Ben Alder is a mountain for the connoisseur and although it can be climbed in a single day by a very fit party it is far more agreeable to make it a two day expedition involving an overnight stop. For this purpose there is, on the east side of Ben Alder, a conveniently situated open bothy which is sturdy and weatherproof although all necessary food, fuel and bedding must be brought.
     Cross the railway line just south of Dalwhinnie station and walk along the private road which hugs the north bank

Ben Alder

of Loch Ericht until you reach Benalder Lodge; a distance of six miles. Keep on the road as it winds steeply through the forest to break out on to the open hillside at a height of 1,500 ft. Just before you reach Loch Pattack and a small plantation on the right hand side of the road you will see a ramshackled wooden hut and a path striking off west across the heather and peat. Follow this path which leads to the south side of the Chaoil-reidhe river and after two more miles to a bridge over this river. Cross over the bridge and in a short distance you arrive at Culra Lodge bothy where you are to spend the night.

As Scottish bothies go Culra Lodge is five star with glazed windows, a table and box type bunk beds. The box beds are useful for keeping out the mice but be sure to hang up all your food from the roof timbers or little will remain in the morning. I know from experience!

Leave Culra Lodge early next morning and walk up the glen towards the Ben Alder—Beinn Bheoil horseshoe. If there is a big river flowing cross the burn by the bridge and keep to the south bank. After one mile a path branches off on the left and leads to Loch a' Bhealaich Bheithe which is set under the steep east facing corries of Ben Alder.

Climb the easy slopes to gain the north shoulder of Beinn Bheoil, 3,333 ft, and enjoy a traverse of the knobbly ridge over the south summit of Sron Coire nah—Iolaire to a bealach at 2,750 ft. Down the glen to the south you can see an inlet of Loch Ericht called Alder Bay where there is another sound, but haunted, bothy. Amongst the rocks on the steep slopes above Alder Bay is Cluny's Cage, a hideout where Bonnie Prince Charlie took refuge in 1746.

Scramble up the rocky hillside to the west of the bealach and thereby gain the almost flat summit plateau of Ben Alder. Distant views extend from Bidean nam Bean and Ben Nevis to the Cairngorms while closer at hand is the superb Aonach Beag—Carn Dearg ridge to the north with the Creag Meagaidh range beyond.

Snow lies on the plateau for most of the year and it is an exhilarating walk northwards along the edge of the great cliffs past the summit trig point to the north eastern spur. This narrow ridge is the northern boundary of Coire na Leith—chais and it provides an interesting way down to the Dubh Glen.

At the bottom of the glen you will meet a good path leading back to Culra Lodge. Pick up your sleeping bag and cooking equipment and start the 11 mile walk back to Dalwhinnie. At the end of such a day your feelings of achievement and euphoria will overcome any possible fatigue.

26. *Bidean nam Bian* O.S. Sheet 41. Map Ref.144542.
    Time 6 hours.

Bidean nam Bian is a high and complex mountain which dominates the pass of Glencoe. It throws out ridges and spurs in many directions such as the impressive rock buttresses known as the Three Sisters easily seen on the left when you drive down the main A82 road through Glencoe.

Leave the road at the Meeting of Three Waters and cross the river Coe by a footbridge. A good path now leads up into a narrow hidden valley whose entrance is almost blocked by huge boulders. This is the famous Lost Valley and in spite of impressive rock scenery all round the valley floor is green and provides good pasture. The MacDonalds used to hide cattle in it.

Climb the steep scree slope at the end of the Lost Valley

and reach the main ridge at a height of about 3,000 feet. Follow the ridge north-westwards for half a mile to gain the summit of Bidean. The views are very impressive; north over the Aonach Eagach ridge to the Mamores and the Nevis range, south to Ben Cruachan and Loch Awe, east to Ben Lui and west over Loch Leven to Ardgour and Mull.

Descend north-east down boulder strewn slopes to reach the col under Stob Coire nan Lochan and then regain the Lost Valley and Glen Coe.

Bidean is a serious mountain and the ascent should not be undertaken lightly particularly in winter conditions or thick mist.

27.   *Ben Starav* O.S. Sheet 50. Map Ref. 126427
      Time 6 hours.

From the Kingshouse Hotel in Glen Coe a road runs south behind Buchaille Etive Mor to Loch Etive. Glen Etive is enclosed to the north by the giants of Glen Coe and to the south by a range of most attractive and individual mountains, the most southerly of which is Ben Starav.

As you drive down Glen Etive past Dalness, Ben Starav is unmistakably seen rising to a sharply pointed summit at the head of the loch. Park your car beside the road one mile north of Glenetive House and cross the river by the bridge near Coileitir Farm.

Follow the path alongside the river and after crossing the Allt Mheuran burn start climbing the steep lower slopes of the north ridge of Ben Starav. It is a long pull to the summit of Ben Starav at 3,541 ft but the ridge is always interesting and it is rocky and quite narrow in places. One winter's day my wife and I were climbing Ben Starav through the snow when two tame goats latched on to us at Coileitir Farm and followed us all the way to the summit. We were far more concerned for their condition than our own for by the time we had climbed the mountain and returned to the farm the poor animals were exhausted and frozen. The kind farmer's wife took all four of us into the kitchen for a warm up.

Ben Starav is a particularly good view point for the beautiful and complex peak of Ben Cruachan ten miles away to the south. Unfortunately Ben Cruachan has been spoilt by the construction, by the Hydro-electric Board, of a gigantic pumped storage system on its southern slopes.

Follow the steep north face round to the east and descend to the bealach, at 2,500 ft, under Glas Bheinn Mhor. This mountain is easily climbed by its west ridge and you can continue beyond the summit at 3,258 ft to the bealach under Stob Coir'an Albannaich. Now follow the glen north for three miles as it gradually descends to Coileitir Farm.

28. *Ben Lawers* O.S. Sheet 51. Map Ref. 635414.
Time 6 hours.

This fine mountain rises to a height of nearly 4,000 feet above Loch Tay in Perthshire. It is one of a group of six mountains which could be traversed in a single day but I advise you to reserve it for a more gentle excursion in Summer. Then you can walk lazily round the grassy ridges enjoying the flowers, picking bilberries and savouring the view.

From the village of Lawers beside Loch Tay walk up the path beside the stream and then climb steep heathery slopes to reach Meall Garbh. The ridge between Meall Garbh and Ben Lawers passes over a fine pointed subsidiary peak called An Stuc which is not named on the O.S. map. The ridge is rocky and broken in places and on the east side the slopes drop precipiously to the aptly named Lochan nan Cat.

Ben Lawers at 3,984 ft is only 16 feet short of the 4,000 foot level and the cairn used to be tall enough to gain this magical height.

You may descend the easy grass slopes almost anywhere to the south to reach Loch Tay or you may wish to continue along the ridge to Beinn Ghlas. If you decide on the latter it will add about an hour to your day as you need to descend 600 feet to a low col and then climb up another 400 feet to Beinn Ghlas. The descent from Beinn Ghlas is also easy in almost any direction.

29. *Ben More and Stobinian* O.S. Sheet 51.
     Map Ref. 825040. Time 6 hours.

Ben More rises to a perfect cone 3,843 ft high which can be seen towering into the sky above Crianlarich as you

Ben More and Stobinian

drive south through Tyndrum on the A82. It is in fact the highest peak in Britain south of Ben Lawers and it is very accessible to the walker. Ben More is linked to another giant, Stobinian 3,821 ft, by a beautifully symmetrical sweep of ridge descending to a bealach. Stobinian too is conically shaped with steep sides but it has its top cut off leaving a flat summit.

Leave the Killin road two miles east of Crianlarich at Benmore farm. A path which starts beside the burn ascends the ever steepening northern slopes of Ben More. The climb is relentless but easy, being mainly over grass although above the 3,000 ft level it passes some rock outcrops. In winter these slopes are often covered in hard frozen snow. Of course an ice axe would be essential in these conditions and crampons could save hours of step cutting.

In misty weather just keep on going upwards and sooner or later you will arrive at the summit trig point.

The major effort of the day is now over and you can enjoy a leisurely spell with the whole of the Southern Highlands spread out below. Close at hand you have an eagle's view of the attractive range of Munros above

Glen Falloch to the south of Cruach Ardrain.

Stobinian is only a mile away to the south but first you must descend 1,000 ft to the Bealach-eadar-dha Beinn before climbing to the summit. Now descend due west down appallingly steep but easy slopes to reach the water-shed at the head of Benmore Glen, a descent of over 2,000 ft. Follow the burn as it rushes northwards down the glen and in two miles you will arrive back at the farm

Ben Lui

30. *Ben Lui Horseshoe* O.S. Sheet 50. Map Ref. 265263. Time 8-9 hours.

Ben Lui is the principal peak of a compact group of four Munros on the Perthshire — Argyllshire border. It rises gracefully to a conical summit 3,708 feet high and in winter the north-east face collects much snow and gives a magnificent route for the serious mountaineer.

Leave the A82 between Crianlarich and Tyndrum at the point where the Land Rover track from Cornish Farm meets the road. Follow this track to the farm, cross the river by a bridge and make your way up the easy slopes to the summit ridge of Beinn Dubhcraig. Once you have gained this height you can enjoy a delightful undulating walk over Ben Oss to Ben Lui. Everything about Ben Lui marks it as the perfect peak. As you ascend the ever steepening south ridge the summit towers above you and cliffs fall away to the east. The summit cairn is poised on the edge of the north face and it commands extensive views of the southern highlands.

When you have drunk your fill from the summit of Ben Lui descend to the low col on the south east side of the mountain. From here it is a short walk to bag your fourth Munro of the day, Ben a' Chleibh. Return to the low col and descend easy slopes to the main road 5 miles from Dalmally.

If you wish to return again to Cononish Farm it is possible to descend the northern spur of Ben Lui over the Ciochan and thence down to the glen. However this route should only be attempted in clear weather because it is easy to mistake the main spur for a smaller one that ends over the cliffs. In bad conditions the safest way is to return down the south east ridge and then swing north down the glen to Cononish.

31.   *Ben Chonzie* O.S. Sheets 51 & 52. Map Ref. 774309.
      Time 3-4 hours.

Ben Chonzie will give you a pleasant short day's walk in peaceful hill country. Situated in upper Glen Almond between Crieff and Aberfeldy it is ideal for one of those days which starts wet yet clears up at mid-day with the clouds rapidly dispersing to give a brilliant afternoon. Ben Chonzie will give you a new Munro in the bargain and provide an unusual view point for the Perthshire hills. The ascent can in fact be accomplished quickly and safely in almost any conditions because the slopes are gentle and route finding is easy.

Turn off the A822 road at Newtown Bridge eight miles north of Crieff and drive along Glen Almond as far as Auchnafree Farm. Cross the river by the bridge and climb up the heathery slopes in a south westerly direction for 1,250 ft to gain the top of the unnamed flat topped mountain to the east of Ben Chonzie. Now descend eastwards to the broad bealach overlooking Lochan Vaine. Climb the steep but easy east facing slopes of Ben Chonzie following an old fence which leads you to the summit. The cairn, at 3,048 ft, has been built into a horseshoe shaped shelter.

As a variation you can descend the northern slopes of Ben Chonzie directly to the Almond River which is bridged near the cottage of Lechrea. Walk back to Auchnafree along the good track on the north side of the river.

Arran

32. *Goat Fell and the Arran Ridges* O.S. Sheet 69.
Map Ref. 991415. Time 8-9 hours.

Arran is a holiday island. In the summer the ferries from Ardrossan to Brodick and Claonaig to Lochranza are bursting with tourists on the way to Arran for the golf, the walking and the generally relaxed atmosphere.

Apart from Goat Fell the range of mountains in the north of the island is more suited to the all round mountaineer than the inexperienced walker. The ridges are narrow and exposed and scrambling is necessary in several places. The combination of mountains and sea is quite as delightful as in the Cuillin of Skye or on Rhum and, being less remote, you can combine an expedition in the mountains during the day with good living in one of the many excellent hotels in the evening. Parties of geologists are often to be found studying the cliffs and dykes, for the rock structure of Arran is exceedingly complex.

It requires a very long day to cover all the peaks and ridges on Arran so I have selected a moderate walk which includes the ascent of several fine mountains and the traverse of some exposed rock ridges.

From Brodick a road runs north along the east coast of Arran and just before it reaches the charming village and harbour of Corrie it crosses the Corrie Burn. A good path beside the burn ascends the grassy slopes for 1,500 ft and then heads south west to gain the west ridge of Goat Fell at the subsidiary summit of Meall Breac. Follow the broad ridge to the summit cairn of Goat Fell at 2,866 ft, built on enormous slabs of granite which have been defaced, over the years, by the action of thousands of geological hammers.

As you climb up from Corrie the view unfolds to the east and north; islands are dotted around the Clyde Estuary and the Sound of Bute and yachts are busy beating up the blue waters of the Firth. On the west side the slopes fall away steeply to Glen Rosa while beyond rises the spec-

The granite ridges of Arran (Goat Fell on the right)

tacular rock ridge of A' Chir and the sharp pointed Cir Mhor which is your next objective.

Walk due north along the tors of the Stacach ridge to Little Goat Fell. The granite rock is severely decayed and in places it crumbles to sand at a touch. Descend the steep north west ridge to the bealach under Cir Mhor which separates the deep glens of Sannox to the north and Rosa to the south. Look out for basaltic dykes on the ridge.

A narrow path winds its way up the rocks and heather of the steep east face of Cir Mhor. Follow this path to the summit cairn which is perched on a huge granite block at 2,618 ft. The path skirts the Rosa Pinnacle, a jutting prow of granite which is famous for its spectacular and exposed rock climbs. Continue northwards along the ridge to Caisteal Abhail or the 'Castles', another group of granite tors. On the rocky hillside below the summit you will see a large cairn marking a spring of pure water which gushes out of the rocks.

From Caisteal Abhail the ridge turns east and you soon arrive at the impressive gash called Ceum na Callich or Witch's Step. The descent into the step is easy from the south but the way out involves an awkward move up an exposed slab. This move can be by-passed by descending north from the Witch's Step and regaining the ridge a little further on.

After the Witch's Step the ridge becomes broad and easy and it soon peters out at the summit of Suidhe Fhearghas. There is no easy descent straight down into Glen Sannox but the slopes on the north side are gentle and after 1,000 ft you can traverse round to the disused barytes mines and the golf course at the mouth of the glen. A pleasant two mile walk down the coast road takes you back to Corrie.